MW00813431

THE PEGGY LEE SONGBOOK

ISBN 0-7935-7281-9

HAL•LEONARD® CORPORATION

7777 W. BLUEMOUND RD. P.O. BOX 13819 MILWAUKEE, WI 53213

Visit Hal Leonard Online at
www.halleonard.com

THE PEGGY LEE SONGBOOK

CONTENTS

MISS PEGGY LEE

In the words of British jazz critic Peter Clayton, Peggy Lee is "quite simply the finest singer in the history of popular music." That's quite a claim, but Clayton is not alone in his views. Others have called her "a living legend" and "an American tradition." None other than Frank Sinatra said, "Her talent should be studied by all vocalists, and her regal presence is pure elegance and charm."

Most importantly, her illustrious career, spanning over five decades, speaks for itself. Her contributions to American music—not only as a singer, but also as a lyricist, composer, and musical innovator—exemplify popular music at its best through the eras of jazz, blues, swing, Latin, and rock.

She has recorded well over 600 songs and sixty albums, a number of which have become gold records. In addition to her recordings, she has appeared on the great stages of the world, in movies, on television, and on radio.

Peggy Lee's awards range from recognition of her musical achievements to citations for humanitarianism, and include Lifetime Achievement awards from ASCAP (the American Society of Composers, Authors and Publishers) and the Society of Singers, Grammy awards that include Best Female Vocalist and another Lifetime Achievement award, an honorary doctorate in music, an Oscar nomination, a Laurel Award from the motion picture exhibitors, an Audience Award from theatergoers, numerous citations from the Cancer Society, the Heart Fund, the National Brotherhood of Christians and Jews, and hundreds of others.

Miss Lee was born Norma Deloris Egstrom on May 26, 1920, in Jamestown, North Dakota. While growing up she sang in the church choir. She was singing professionally by the time she was fourteen, and within a few years had ventured from Jamestown to Fargo. It was there Norma met Ken Kennedy, program director of radio station WDAY. He was so impressed by her talent that he put her on the air within an hour of meeting her, but decided that the name Norma Egstrom just wouldn't do—so he christened her Peggy Lee.

It was the age of the big band, and in 1936 Miss Lee joined the Jack Wardlow Band, stepping up a few years later to the Will Osborne Band. She traveled to Chicago, Minneapolis, California, and back to Chicago, where she caught the ear of none other than Benny Goodman. He quickly signed her up with his orchestra, arguably the most popular and influential big band ever.

Miss Lee stayed with Goodman from 1941 to 1943. During that time she sang on a number of his hit recordings, including "I Got It Bad and That Ain't Good," "Blues in the Night," "**Somebody Else Is Taking My Place**," and "Jersey Bounce." But the recording that made her a household name was "**Why Don't You Do Right**," in 1942. It was a song she had chosen, and it offered a glimpse of the independence and creative sense that have driven her entire career.

In 1943 Miss Lee married Dave Barbour, Goodman's guitarist, and retired from performing. She gave birth to a daughter, Nicki, and was intent on being a full-time wife and mother.

During this period, a pastime from her own childhood resurfaced, making a far bigger impact on her life than she might ever have imagined. "I've been making up verses to tunes as far back as I can remember," she said. Her first memories of doing so date back to her early childhood in Jamestown.

As a married woman, she was washing dishes one day and thinking how much she loved her husband, and the words for "What More Can a Woman Do?" came pouring out of her thoughts. When Barbour came home that evening, she told him the lyric, and in a few hours they had the first of the numerous songs they wrote together. It was the beginning of Miss Lee's career as a professional songwriter—a career that would produce over 500 songs, many of them hits.

But songwriting wasn't enough, and it was Dave Barbour who first realized it. He told her that she had too much talent as a singer not to use it to its fullest. He said that if she stopped singing, she would regret it someday. As Miss Lee later recalled, "I cried at the time, but David was right."

Her decision to resume singing came at the right time: Columbia Records asked her to record two songs for a four-disc set called *New American Jazz*. Her contributions—"Ain't Goin' No Place" and "That Old Feeling"—cemented her position in the highest ranks of American singers.

It was with Barbour that Miss Lee wrote many of her early hits, including "I Don't Know Enough About You," "**Mañana**," and "**It's a Good Day**." In the years following, she has written a wide and varied range of musical material with some of the greatest musicians and songwriters in America, including Duke Ellington, Harold Arlen, Johnny Mandel, Cy Coleman, Victor Young, Sonny Burke, Dave Grusin, and Quincy Jones.

In writing her own material long before it was fashionable for singers to do so, Miss Lee also established herself as a trend-setter. Another trend she helped establish was the use of Latin rhythms in American popular music, beginning with "Mañana" in 1948, through her unique pop/Latin take on Rodgers and Hart's classic "**Lover**" in 1952, to her epoch-making album *Latin ala Lee!* in 1960.

The 1950s found Miss Lee's career expanding to include the world of motion pictures. In 1950 she appeared in *Mr. Music*, with Bing Crosby, among others. She played opposite Danny Thomas in the 1953 remake of *The Jazz Singer*, and also wrote and performed the song "**This Is a Very Special Day**" for the movie. And her portrayal of Rosie, an alcoholic blues singer, in *Pete Kelly's Blues* (1955) earned her an Oscar nomination as Best Supporting Actress.

Perhaps Miss Lee's proudest moment in the movies came with Walt Disney's feature-length cartoon *Lady and the Tramp* (1954). In addition to writing the songs with Sonny Burke, she gave voice to no fewer than four of the roles in the picture: the mischievous Siamese cats Si and Am ("**The Siamese Cat Song**"), the young human mother Darling ("La La Lu"), and the down-on-her-luck ex-showdog Peg ("**He's a Tramp**"). That last character, a vampy Pekinese, was originally named Mamie, but since Mamie Eisenhower was the First Lady at the time, Walt asked Miss Lee whether she'd mind if the character were renamed after her. She was delighted. "The animators even asked me to walk for them as a model for Peg's walk."

Although Miss Lee has always regarded working with Walt Disney as "one of the greatest honors of my life," there is a bittersweet ending to the story. Miss Lee maintained in the years following that her contributions to the film weren't properly acknowledged. The matter went to court, where things were ultimately decided in her favor.

Her involvement with movies didn't end when she stopped playing parts. She has written words or music for a number of motion pictures, including *Johnny Guitar* ("**Johnny Guitar**"), *About Mrs. Leslie, Tom Thumb,* and *The Heart Is a Lonely Hunter.*

In 1958 Miss Lee released one of her biggest and most influential hits, "**Fever**." The sparse, stylish accompaniment of bass, drums, and finger snaps was her idea. Johnny Mandel may have had this song in mind when he called Miss Lee's singing style "minimalist" (a compliment, by the way, and a label with which Miss Lee agrees). But that word isn't restricted to the cool fire of this song; no matter the mood or tempo, her hallmark has always been subtlety of phrasing, color, and characterization.

Whether or not "**I'm a Woman**" remains current with the ever-shifting roles of women in society, there is no doubt that Miss Lee's 1962 recording of the song helped set the tone for the women's movement that followed. Is her impassioned performance merely the work of a consummate artist, or is there a bit of self-portrait in this musical picture of a thoroughly capable, yet utterly feminine, modern woman?

"When rock 'n' roll came along, it scared me to death," Miss Lee has said. Nevertheless, she was one of the first of the established singers to recognize the worth and talent of many of the upcoming rock songwriters. She began including their material in her performances and recordings. For example, she recorded "A Hard Day's Night" less than a year after The Beatles first released it. Some time later, Paul McCartney thanked her by writing the song "Let's Love" for her, which she recorded for the 1974 album of the same name.

The tables have continued to turn, as a younger generation of performers, including Madonna and k.d. lang, now attests to Miss Lee's influence on them.

Visionary that she is, Miss Lee has often had to fight with record company executives to release the music she believes in. It was that way in 1952 with "Lover." And it was that way again in 1969 with "**Is That All There Is**." She pondered the words to the song long and deeply before deciding to record it. "I must believe in a song to sing it," said Miss Lee, who through the years has refused to ever sing a lyric devoid of hope. Her interpretation of this song answers the question posed by the title with a certain "Oh no, there's more!" For those listeners who missed that message and wrote her letters of concern, she wrote each one back personally to make her feelings absolutely clear. "I want everyone to know this is *'not* all there is'."

Miss Lee has continued to record and perform. In 1983 she starred in the one-woman show *Peg* on Broadway, and despite several bouts with illness, she has never ceased performing in concert around the world.

She put her life story in writing in *Miss Peggy Lee: An Autobiography* (1989), and it climbed to #1 on the London *Times* best-seller list. But it must be said that the publication of that book was premature; the life story of Peggy Lee is still being written.

Surely by now she could rest on her past accomplishments. What drives her to continue? She offers this explanation: "I am guided in life by the grand essentials. Something to do, something to love, and something to hope for."

LOUIS ARMSTRONG — FRANK SINATRA — BING CROSBY

SELECTED ALBUMS

A&M
Mirrors

Atlantic
Let's Love

Capitol
Peggy Lee
Peggy Lee's Greatest
Rendezvous with Peggy Lee
My Best to You
The Man I Love
Jump for Joy
Music of Jerome Kern
Things Are Swingin'
Music of South Pacific
I Like Men!
Happy Holiday
Beauty and the Beat
Latin ala Lee!
All Aglow Again
Pretty Eyes
The Folks Who Live on the Hill
Broadway a la Lee
Christmas Carousel
Olé ala Lee!
Basin Street East
If You Go
Blue Cross Country
Bewitching-Lee!
Sugar 'n' Spice
I'm a Woman
Mink Jazz
In Love Again!
In the Name of Love
Pass Me By
Then Was Then: Now Is Now
Guitars ala Lee
Big $pender
Extra Special
Somethin' Groovy
Hits of Peggy Lee
A Natural Woman
Greatest!
Is That All There Is?
Bridge over Troubled Water
Make It with You
Where Did They Go?
Norma Deloris Egstrom from Jamestown,
   North Dakota
Capitol Collectors Series, Vol. 1: The Early Years
P's & Q's
Love Held Lightly: Rare Songs by Harold Arlen
Classics
Best of the Capitol Years

CEMA
Fever & Other Hits

Chesky
Moments Like This

Columbia
Benny Goodman and Peggy Lee
Benny Goodman Presents Peggy Lee
Benny Goodman with Peggy Lee
Miss Peggy Lee
Sings with Benny Goodman

Curb
All-Time Greatest Hits

Decca/MCA
Black Coffee
Song in an Intimate Style
Songs from Lady and the Tramp
Songs from Pete Kelly's Blues
Miss Wonderful
The Fabulous Peggy Lee
Lover
Selections from White Christmas
Sea Shells
The Jazz Singer
Dream Street
Best of Peggy Lee
The Best of Peggy Lee
Peggy Lee

DRG
Close Enough for Love

Glendale
You Can Depend on Me

Hindsight
Uncollected Peggy Lee (1948)

Jasmine
If I Could Be with You

Laserlight
With the Dave Barbour Band
Jazz Collector Edition

RCA/MusicMasters
Sings the Blues
There'll Be Another Spring
Peggy Lee Songbook

Pair
Seductive

Pioneer
Quintessential

Polydor
Peggy Lee: Live in London

Viper's Nest
Why Don't You Do Right?

MISS PEGGY LEE WITH HER FRIENDS

NAT KING COLE — JUNE CHRISTY — MEL TORME — STAN KENTON

RONALD REAGAN

WOODY HERMAN

CHARLES BOYER

DANNY THOMAS

CHARLES COLLINGWOOD (CBS)

ROBERT PRESTON

TONY BENNETT

JACK WEBB

BENNY GOODMAN

FRANK MORGAN — VICTOR MOORE

CHARLES COBURN

BUGS BAER — TOOTS SHOR — JACKIE GLEASON

MISS PEGGY LEE WITH HER FRIENDS

ARTHUR TREACHER — JIMMY DURANTE — GREER GARSON

PAUL McCARTNEY

AL JOLSON

PERRY COMO — PAULA KELLY

DR. JONAS SALK

ARTHUR GODFREY

ALICE FAYE

GEORGE BURNS — JACK CARTER

HENRY CABOT LODGE

JEFF CHANDLER

DON AMECHE — DONALD VORHEESE
RUDY VALLEE — ROBERTA PETERS

LIBERACE — DAVE BARBOUR

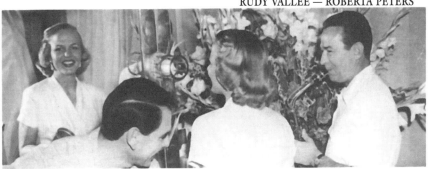

DAVE BARBOUR — JIMMY DORSEY and MIRROR

Big Spender

from SWEET CHARITY

Words by DOROTHY FIELDS
Music by CY COLEMAN

D.S. al Coda

Fever

Words and Music by JOHN DAVENPORT
and EDDIE COOLEY

Verse 3 Romeo loved Juliet
Juliet she felt the same,
When he put his arms around her, he said,
"Julie, baby you're my flame."

Chorus Thou givest fever, when we kisseth
Fever with my flaming youth,
Fever – I'm afire
Fever, yea I burn forsooth.

Verse 4 Captain Smith and Pocahantas
Had a very mad affair,
When her Daddy tried to kill him, she said,
"Daddy-o don't you dare."

Chorus Give me fever, with his kisses,
Fever when he holds me tight.
Fever – I'm his Missus
Oh Daddy won't you treat him right.

Verse 5 Now you've listened to my story
Here's the point that I have made:
Chicks were born to give you fever
Be it fahrenheit or centigrade.

Chorus They give you fever when you kiss them,
Fever if you live and learn.
Fever – till you sizzle
What a lovely way to burn.

Golden Earrings

from the Paramount Picture GOLDEN EARRINGS

Words by JAY LIVINGSTON and RAY EVANS
Music by VICTOR YOUNG

One day a gyp-sy showed me gold - en ear - rings that he wished to sell.

He's a Tramp

from Walt Disney's LADY AND THE TRAMP

Words and Music by PEGGY LEE
and SONNY BURKE

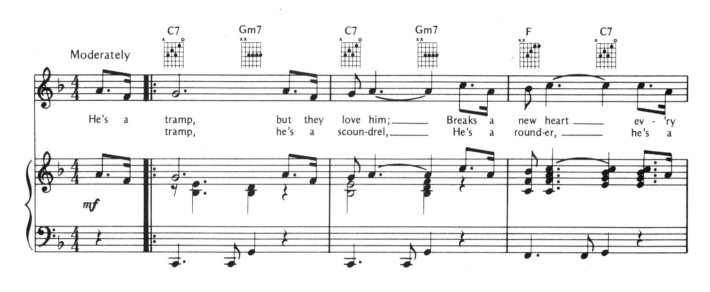

8va
lower

I Love Being Here with You

Words and Music by PEGGY LEE
and BILL SCHLUGER

Moderately, with a beat

Is That All There Is

Words and Music by JERRY LEIBER
and MIKE STOLLER

I'm a Woman

Words and Music by JERRY LEIBER
and MIKE STOLLER

Spoken:

I can wash out forty-four pairs of socks and have them hangin' out on the line,
I can rub and scrub till this old house is shinin' like a dime,
If you come to me sickly, you know I'm gonna make you well,
I can stretch a greenback dollar bill from here to kingdom come.

I can starch and iron two dozen shirts before you can count from one to nine,
Feed the baby, grease the car and powder my face at the same time,
If you come to me hexed up, you know I'm gonna break the spell,
I can play the numbers, pay my bills, and still end up with some.

I can scoop up a great big dipper full of lard from the drippin's can,
Get all dressed up, go out and swing till four a.m. and then
If you come to me hungry, I'm gonna fill you full o' grits,
I got a twenty dollar gold piece says there ain't nothing I can't do.

Throw it in the skillet, go out and do my shopping and be back before it melts in the pan,
Lay down at five, jump up at six and start all over again,
If it's love you're lackin', I'll kiss you and give you the shiverin' fits,
I can make a dress out of a feedbag and I can make a man out of you,

Sung: 'Cause I'm a

wom - an, ___ dou-ble u - o - m - a - n. ___ I'll say it a -

gain. gain. 'Cause I'm a wom - an, ___

dou - ble u - o - m - a - n. ___

It's a Good Day

Words and Music by PEGGY LEE
and DAVE BARBOUR

Lover

from the Paramount Picture LOVE ME TONIGHT

Words by LORENZ HART
Music by RICHARD RODGERS

Moderately

Lyrics:
When you held your hand to my heart, dear, you did some-thing grand to my heart, and we played the scene to per-fec-tion, _____ though we did-n't have time to re-hearse. _____

Lov - er, ____ please be ten - der. ____ When you're ten - der, ____ fears de - part. ____ Lov - er, ____ I sur - ren - der ____ to my heart. ____ heart. ____

8va basso

Johnny Guitar

Words by PEGGY LEE
Music by VICTOR YOUNG

Just One of Those Things

Words and Music by
COLE PORTER

Mañana

Words and Music by PEGGY LEE
and DAVE BARBOUR

The fau - cet she is drip - ping and the
moth - er's al - ways work - ing; she's

See additional lyrics

fence she's fall - ing down. My
work - ing ver - y hard. But

pock - et needs some mon - ey so I
ev - 'ry time she looks for me I'm

Additional Lyrics

3. Oh, once I had some money but I gave it to my friend.
   He said he'd pay me double, it was only for a lend.
   But he said a little later that the horse she was so slow.
   Why he gave the horse my money is something I don't know.

4. My brother took his suitcase and he went away to school.
   My father said he only learn'd to be a silly fool.
   My father said that I should learn to make a chili pot.
   But then I burn'd the house down the chili was too hot.

5. The window she is broken and the rain is coming in.
   If someone doesn't fix it I'll be soaking to my skin.
   But if we wait a day or two the rain may go away.
   And we don't need a window on such a sunny day.

Mr. Wonderful
from the Musical MR. WONDERFUL

Words and Music by JERRY BOCK,
LARRY HOLOFCENER and GEORGE DAVID WEISS

Slowly and expressively

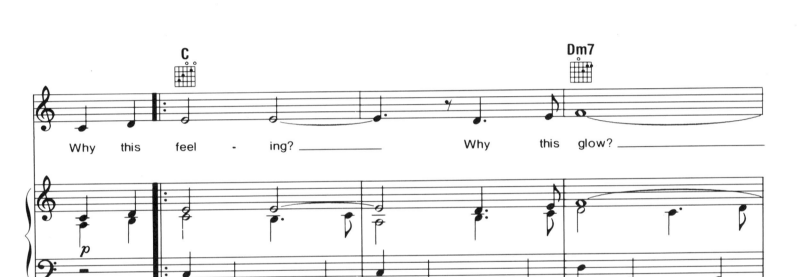

Why this feel - ing? _____ Why this glow? _____

_____ Why the thrill when you say, "Hel - lo!"? _____

The Siamese Cat Song
from Walt Disney's LADY AND THE TRAMP

Words and Music by PEGGY LEE
and SONNY BURKE

We are Si - am-ese with ver - y dain -ty claws.

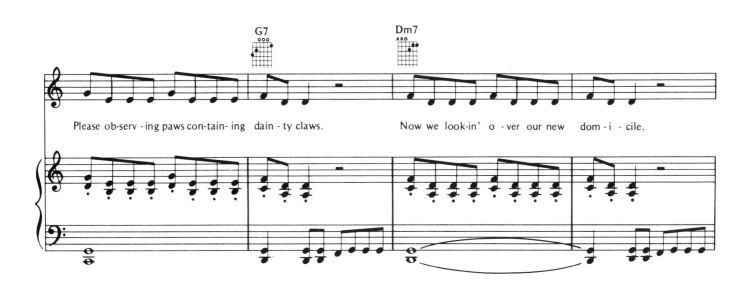

Please ob-serv -ing paws con-tain- ing dain - ty claws. Now we look-in' o -ver our new dom-i - cile.

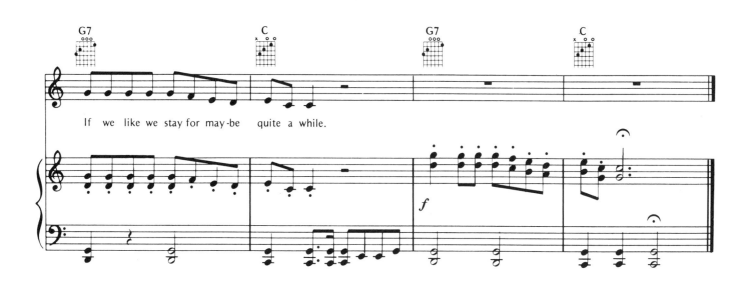

If we like we stay for may -be   quite a while.

Somebody Else Is Taking My Place

Words and Music by DICK HOWARD,
BOB ELLSWORTH and RUSS MORGAN

This Is a Very Special Day

Words and Music by
PEGGY LEE

Why Don't You Do Right
(Get Me Some Money, Too!)

By JOE McCOY

Them There Eyes

Words and Music by MACEO PINKARD,
WILLIAM TRACY and DORIS TAUBNER

Moderately, with a Swing beat